AROUND the WORLD MYSTERY MAZES

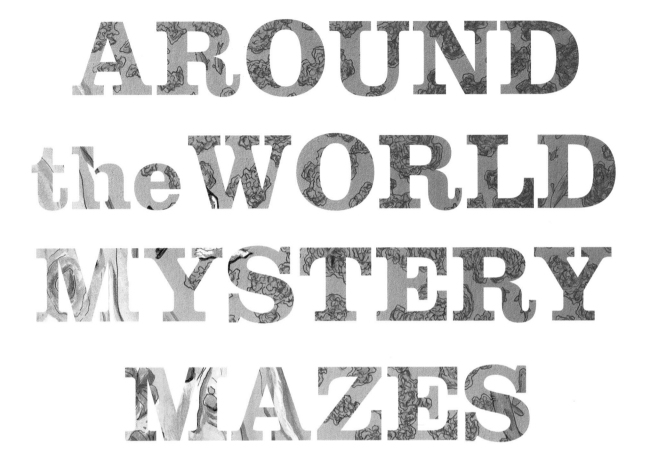

by Roger Moreau

Sterling Publishing Co., Inc.
New York

**This book is dedicated to
Gayle, Marc, Kevin, Lisa, and David.**

2 4 6 8 10 9 7 5 3 1

Published by Sterling Publishing Co., Inc.
387 Park Avenue South, New York, NY 10016
© 2003 by Roger Moreau
Distributed in Canada by Sterling Publishing
C/o Canadian Manda Group, One Atlantic Avenue, Suite 105
Toronto, Ontario, Canada M6K 3E7
Distributed in Great Britain and Europe by Chris Lloyd at Orca Book
Services, Stanley House, Fleets Lane, Poole BH15 3AJ, England
Distributed in Australia by Capricorn Link (Australia) Pty. Ltd.
P.O. Box 704, Windsor, NSW 2756, Australia

Printed in Hong Kong

0-8069-9288-3

Contents

A Note on the Suggested Use of This Book 4

Introduction 5

Stonehenge 7

The Search for the Mayan "Rosetta Stone" 8

The Search Continued 10

The Mayan "Rosetta Stone" 12

The Olmec Head 14

Easter Island Sculptures 15

The Great Pyramid 16

The Search for the Ark of the Covenant 18

The Ark of the Covenant 20

Enter the Money Pit 22

The Money Pit Continued 23

The Lost Colony of Roanoke 24

The *Mary Celeste* 26

The Bermuda Triangle 28

Amelia Earhart 30

Nessie 32

Big Foot 33

Mallory's Camera 34

The Yeti 36

Noah's Ark 38

Shangri-La 40

Roswell's UFO 42

Crop Circles 43

D.B. Cooper 44

The Fountain of Youth 46

Atlantis Island 48

The City of Atlantis 50

Congratulations! 52

Answer Mazes 53

Index 80

A Note on the Suggested Use of This Book

As you work your way through the pages of this book, try not to mark them. This will enable you to take this journey over and over again and will also give your friends a chance to take the same journey you took.

Special Warning: When the way looks too difficult, avoid the temptation to start at the end and work your way backwards. This technique would be a violation of the rules and could result in you becoming lost forever.

Cover Maze: Before you are the objects of a number of unsolved mysteries. Try to find a clear path around these mysteries to the pyramids on the horizon.

Introduction

Throughout history, many events have occurred and great monuments, sculptures, temples, walls, and religious shrines have been constructed that, to some extent, remain unexplained mysteries. How were the pyramids built? What is the meaning of Stonehenge, and what happened to Amelia Earhart? Wouldn't it be wonderful and exciting if someone could go back in time to the actual location of an unsolved mystery and find the answer? Such an adventure would probably be dangerous and require great courage, but think of the satisfaction of knowing the truth.

How did the Olmec people, over 3,000 years ago, move a 40-ton stone over water and rough terrain for 60 miles without modern moving equipment? A similar type of work occurred on remote Easter Island, located in the South Pacific Ocean, where 200 giant stone heads and figures line the coast, some weighing 82 tons and standing 33 feet tall. In the quarry inland were another 700 statues that had never been moved into place along the shoreline. What did these statues represent, and how were they transported from the quarry? These are just two examples of this type of mystery, and no one knows the answers to the questions they present.

More current mysteries have occurred like the disappearances of airplanes and ships in an area known as the Bermuda Triangle, located off the southeastern Atlantic Coast of the United States. Flight 19 is a good example. Five Grumman "Avengers" took off from Fort Lauderdale, Florida on December 5th, 1945 over an area known as the Bermuda Triangle and were never seen again. What happened to them? Emelia Earhart disappeared somewhere over the Pacific during her around-the-world flight in 1937. What happened? D.B. Cooper bailed out over the Columbia River in 1971 with $200,000 of stolen money and has never been seen again. Where's D.B. and where's the money? These are just a few of this type of unsolved mystery. Wouldn't it be fun to know what happened?

You now have a chance to set out on the following pages and investigate these and many more of the great unsolved mysteries of the world.

All you have to do is accept the challenge to explore many dangerous parts of the world as you attempt to get the answers. You'll have to be tenacious to reach difficult locations in order to examine each particular mystery. In addition to those mentioned above are some more mysteries you'll be setting out to examine:

1. Why did the Egyptians leave the capstone off the top of the Great Pyramid?

2. The ancient Mayas sculpted pictures as a language form. What do their pictures mean? What if a sculptured picture could be found with the meaning next to it in a known language, like the Rosetta Stone that was found in Egypt that revealed the meaning of the Egyptian language?

3. What ever happened to the Ark of the Convenant?

4. Is there a great treasure at the bottom of the money pit on Nova Scotia's Oak Island?

5. What happened to the people of Roanoke Island (located off the coast of present-day North Carolina) in the late sixteenth century? The entire colony disappeared and left only a sign with the word "Croatan" on it.

6. The *Mary Celeste* was a sailing ship that set out from New York for Europe in 1872. All aboard disappeared and only the ship was found. What happened?

7. Is there Big Foot, Yeti, and what about Nessie?

8. Is Noah's Ark on top of Mount Ararat?

9. Was there ever or is there now a Shangri-La, that idyllic hideaway where life is almost perfect?

10. What really happened at Roswell, New Mexico, where people claimed a UFO crashed into a farmer's field?

11. Are crop circles a hoax or do aliens from another world create them?

12. Ponce de Leon never found the Fountain of Youth. That doesn't mean there isn't one, does it?

13. Some believe Atlantis sunk into the sea. Did it?

There are many great unsolved mysteries in the world. It would be great if you could explore them all, but that would not be possible. Just remember, it is important that you don't give up, because if you do then that mystery may never be solved. **Good Luck!**

Stonehenge

Starting in 3200 B.C., Stonehenge was built over a period of 1,200 years in Wiltshire, England. Find a clear path to the top of those three Stonehenge stones.

The Search for the Mayan "Rosetta Stone"

Can you find the Mayas' stone tablet, similar to the Egyptians' Rosetta Stone, that will help you decode their language? Begin your search by climbing to the top of this mountain. Climb the ladders and move right or left on the ledges to get up.

Start

The Search Continued

Work your way through the ruins to the temple on the right.

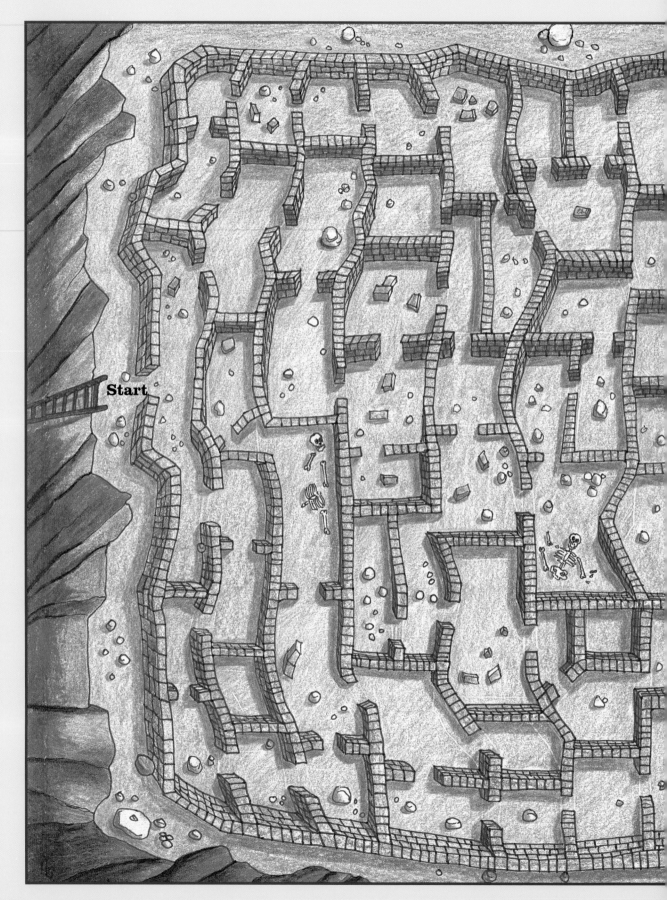

Start

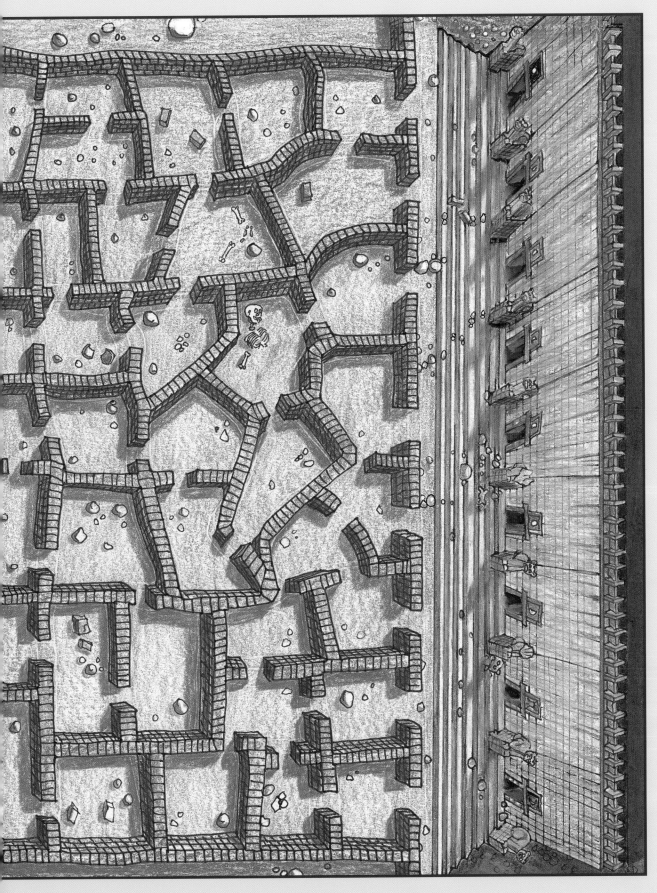

The Mayan "Rosetta Stone"

This special stone, with a picture on the left and its meaning on the right, will reveal the meaning of the Mayan language. Find a clear path to it.

End

The Olmec Head

The quarries were over 60 miles away from where the Olmec heads now rest. How did the Olmecs move them? Find a clear path from the quarry to the Olmec head.

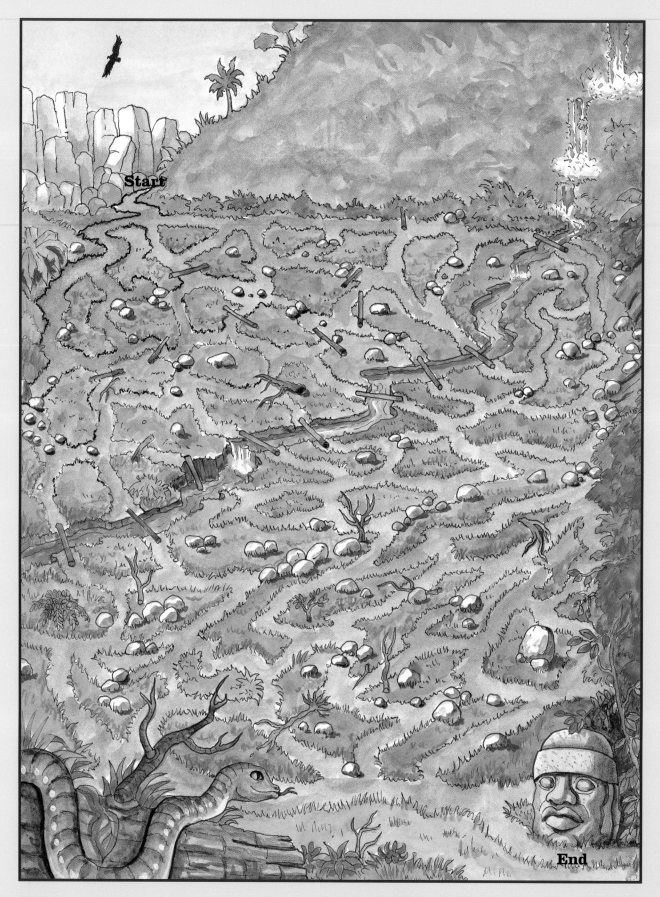

Easter Island Sculptures

These ancient sculptures cover Easter Island. Why were they made? What is their meaning? Visit each sculpture along the path without backtracking.

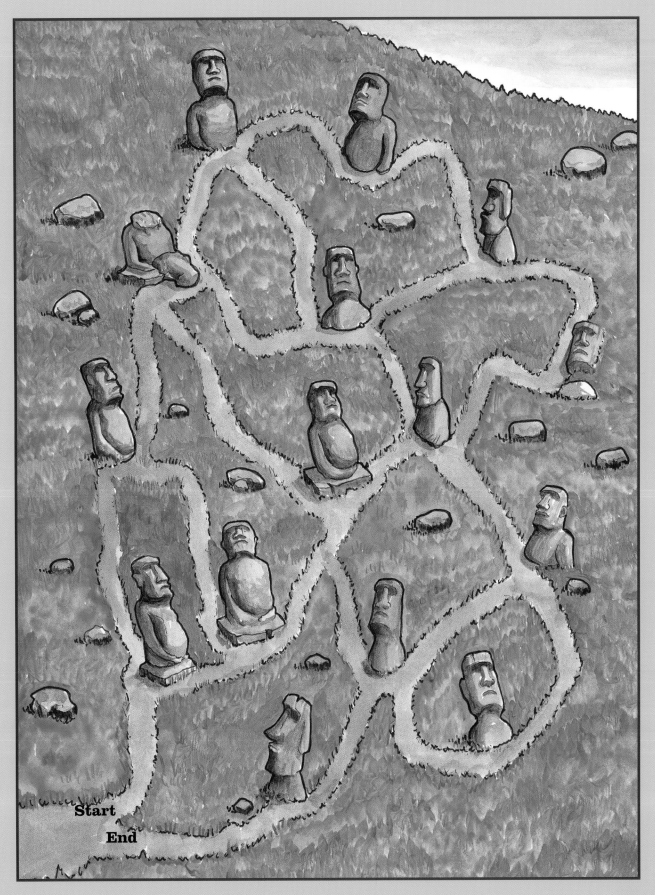

The Great Pyramid

Climb the Great Pyramid. Wherever a block on the pyramid is missing, you can move onto that square and then move right, left, or straight ahead to climb the pyramid. See the example on the scroll on how to move.

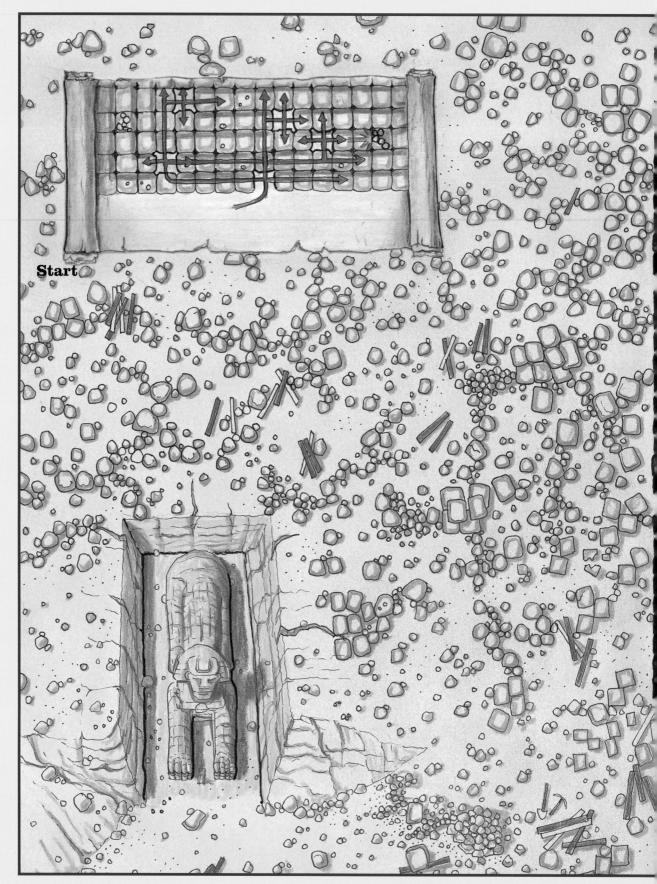

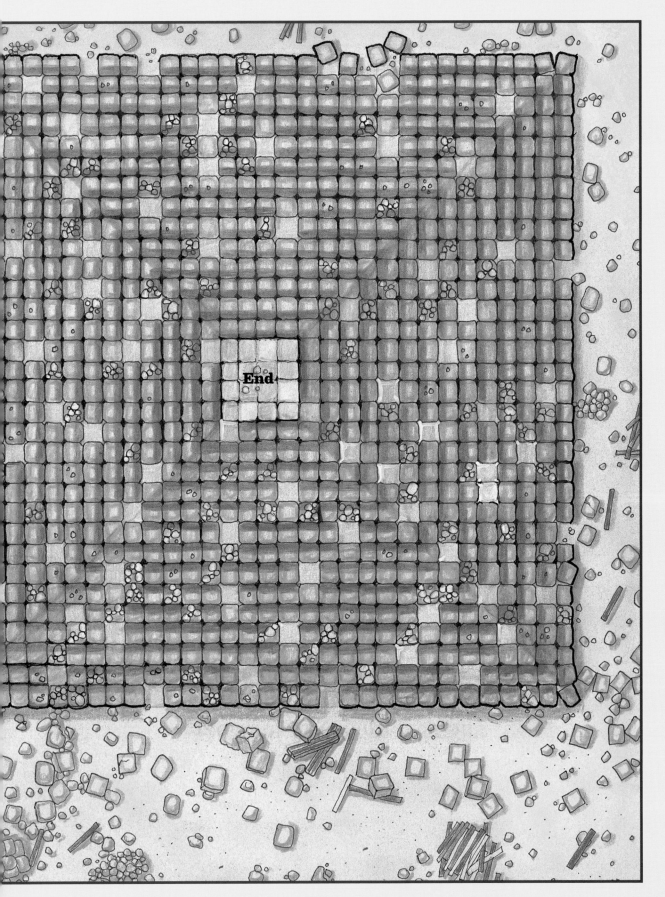

End

The Search for the Ark of the Covenant

Find your way to the correct hole opening.

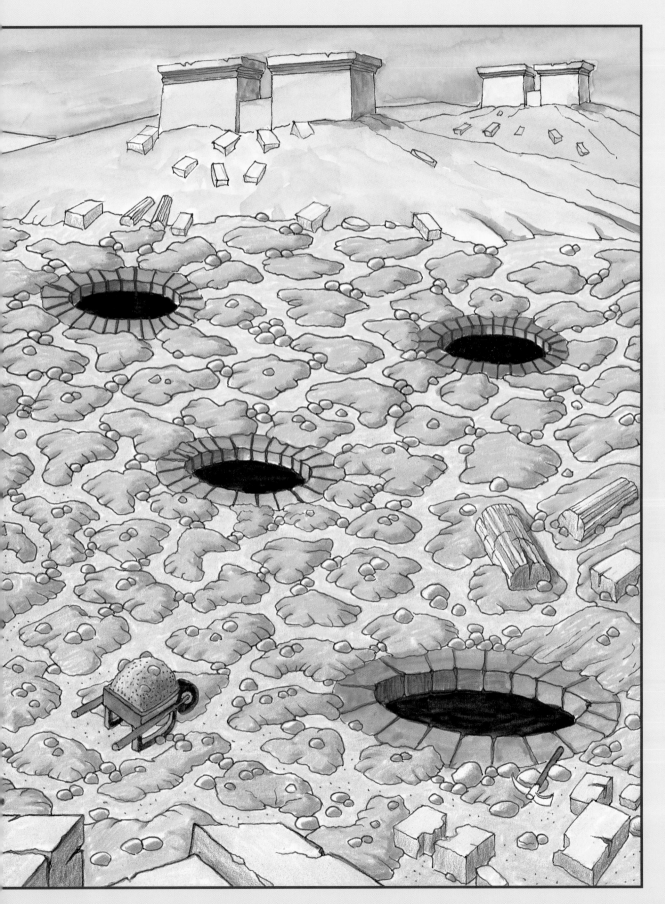

The Ark of the Covenant

Find a clear path to the Ark of the Covenant without disturbing the snakes.

End

Enter the Money Pit

There may be a treasure chest at the bottom of this money pit. One of the keys may open the treasure chest. Pick up each key as you work your way through the money pit. Do not backtrack or go through the same opening twice.

Start

The Money Pit Continued

Continue picking up keys. Do not backtrack or go through the same opening twice. End at the bottom of the pit.

End

The Lost Colony of Roanoke

Roanoke was founded in 1587 with 90 men, 17 women, and 9 children. The entire colony was missing in 1590, but the word "Croatan" was found carved on a post. Find a clear path to the post.

Start

The *Mary Celeste*

The *Mary Celeste* set sail for Europe in 1872. She was found adrift with no one on board. What happened? Find a pathway between the waves to the *Mary Celeste*.

Start

End

The Bermuda Triangle

Flight 19, consisting of five Grumman TBM "Avenger" aircraft, was lost on December 5, 1945 in the Bermuda Triangle. Find a clear way to the five aircraft and touch each plane.

Amelia Earhart

Amelia Earhart and her navigator, Fred Noonan, were trying to find Howland Island in the Pacific to refuel on her around-the-world flight in 1937. She disappeared. Try to find her airplane by finding a clear way from the island to the plane.

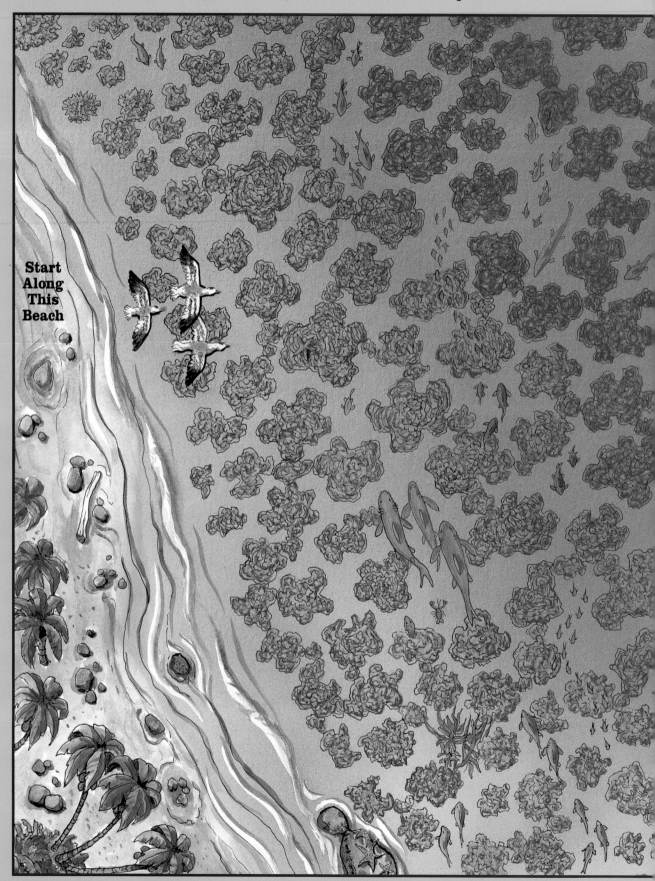

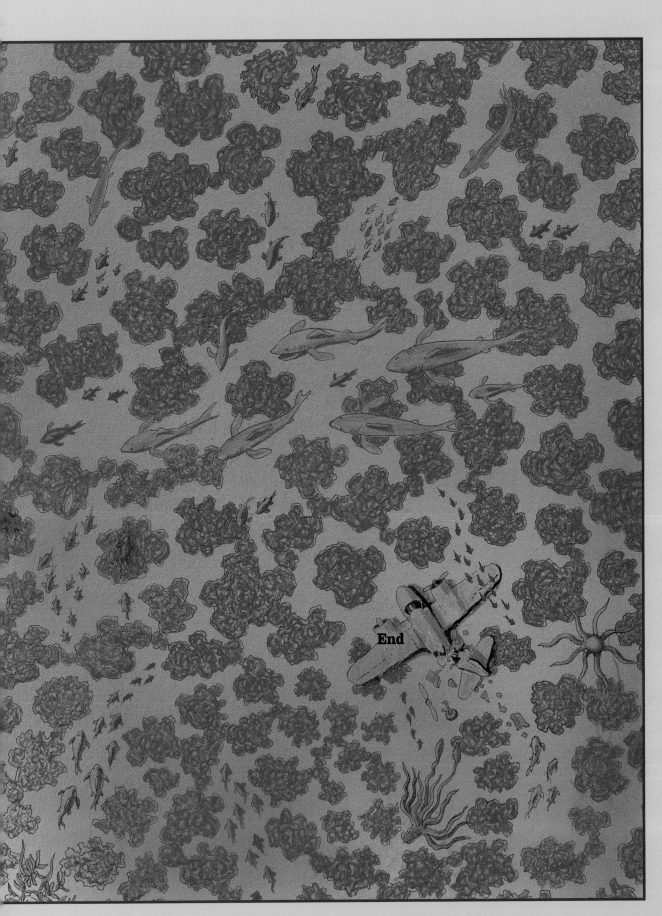

End

Nessie

Do you have the courage to look for the Loch Ness monster—known affectionately as Nessie? Find a clear path down to where she is.

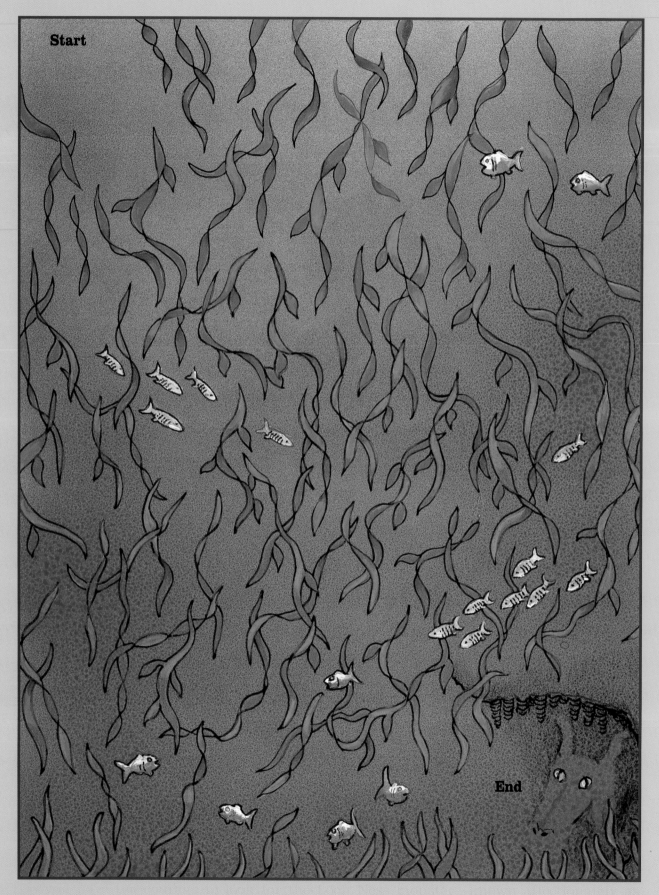

Big Foot

There he is! Find a clear path and get to Big Foot before he gets away . . . again.

Mallory's Camera

Did George Mallory and Andrew Irvine reach the summit of Mount Everest? Finding his camera should solve the mystery. Climb to the location where Mallory's body was found by staying on the snow and see if you can find his camera.

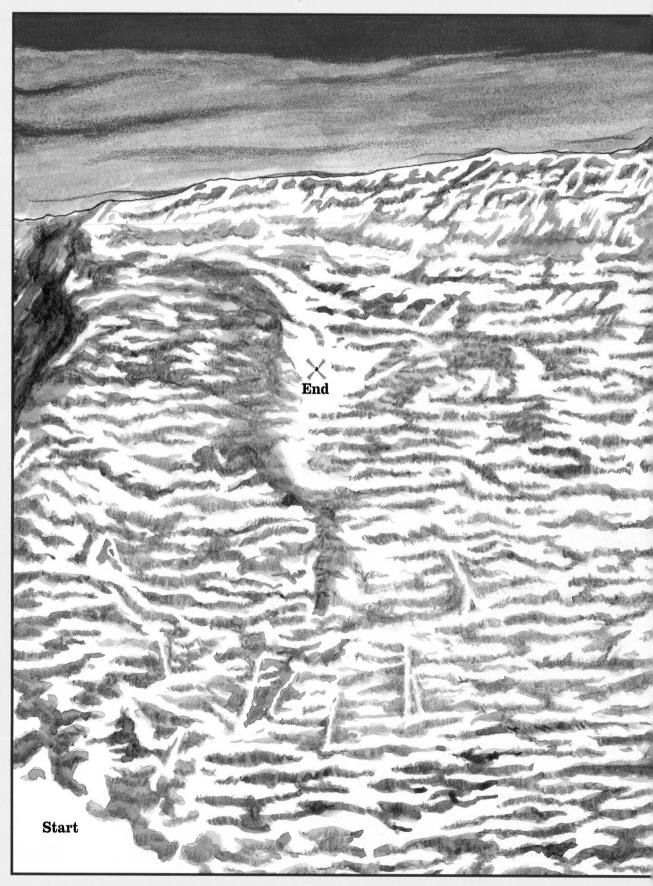

The Yeti

Large footprints have been found in the high Himalayas. Could they belong to a large hairy beast called a Yeti? Follow the tracks to the correct snow cave to find out.

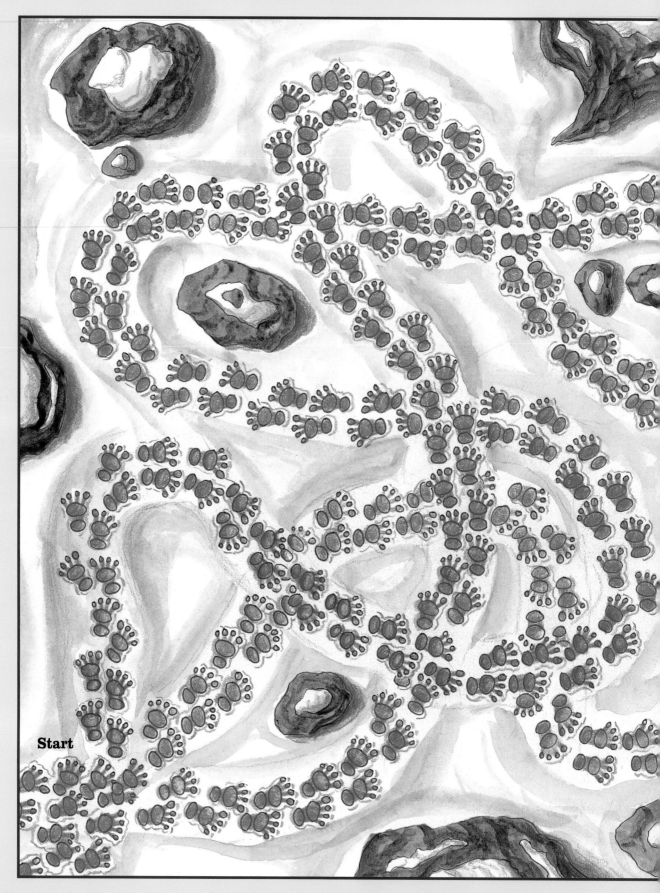

Start

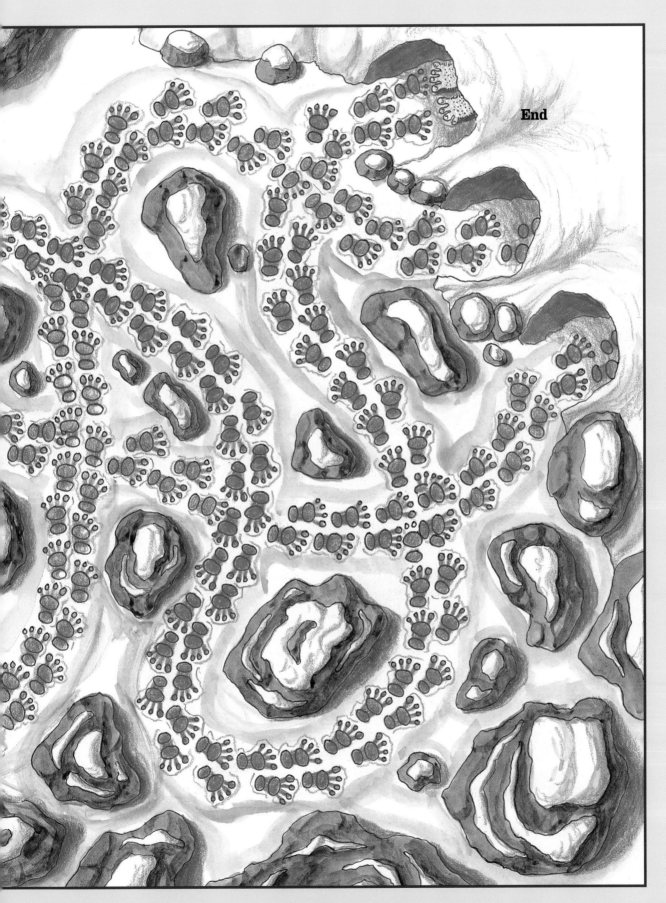

End

Noah's Ark

Somewhere at the top of Mount Ararat could be Noah's Ark. Find a clear path to what looks like a boat to find out.

Start

End

Shangri-La

Is there such a place as "Shangri-La"? That city at the top of the mountain looks like there could be. Find your way to the top to find out.

Start

End

Roswell's UFO

Check out this UFO that has crashed into a farmer's field in Roswell, New Mexico to see whether there are any aliens inside. Find a clear path.

Crop Circles

Who made these crop circles? Find your way to the center of both circles and end at the center of the one on the right. Don't backtrack.

D.B. Cooper

D.B. Cooper leaped out of an airplane over the Columbia River in 1971 with $200,000 in his possession. He was never seen again, but a bundle of $20 bills was found in

Start

1980. Hike through the forest and pick up each bill without backtracking and reach D.B. Cooper under the parachute.

The Fountain of Youth

Ponce de Leon never found the Fountain of Youth. Now you can. Just swim past all the alligators to the fountain across the pond.

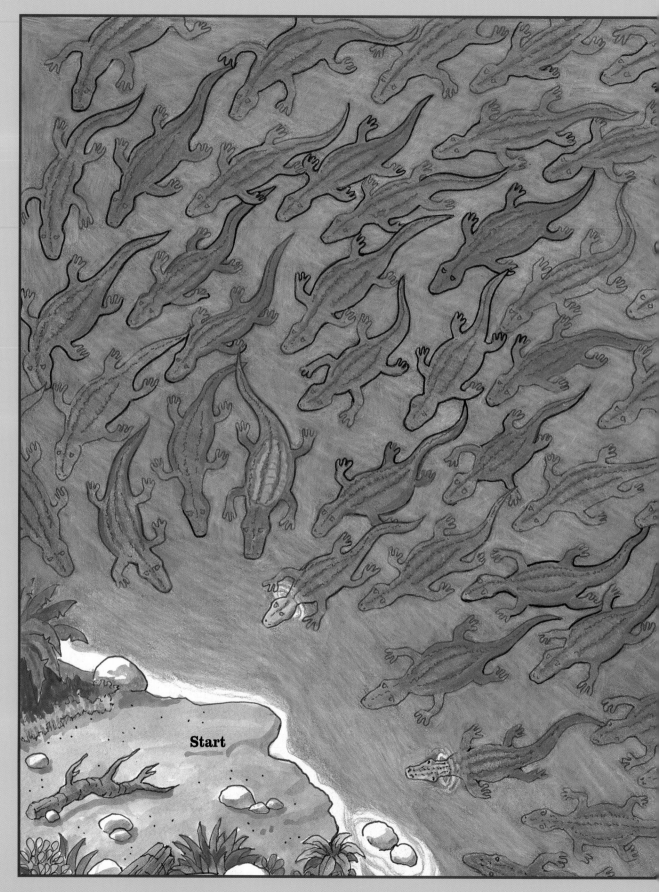

Start

End

Atlantis Island

The great city of Atlantis was on one of these islands when it sank into the sea. But which island? Find a pathway between the waves that will enable you to reach the correct island.

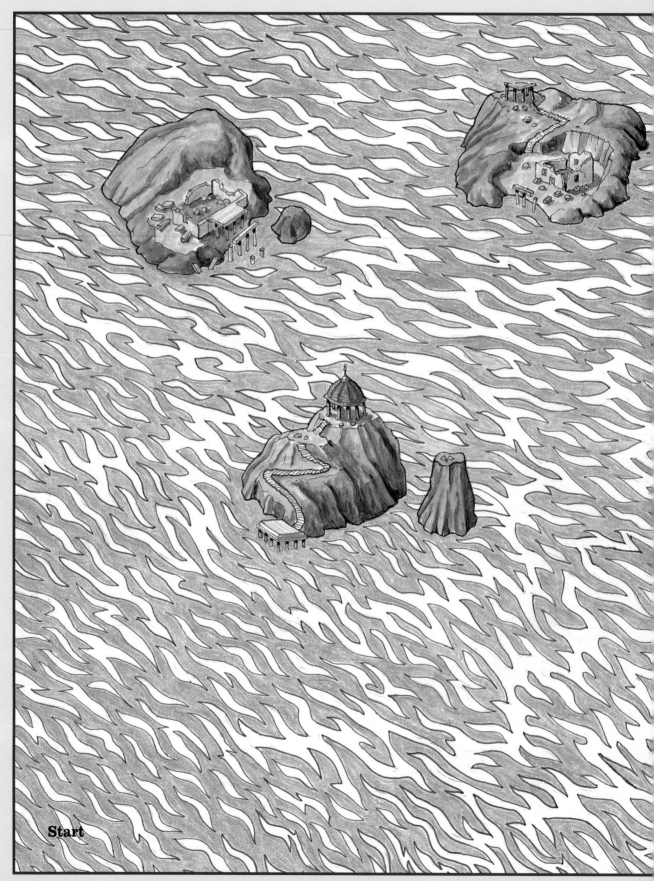

Start

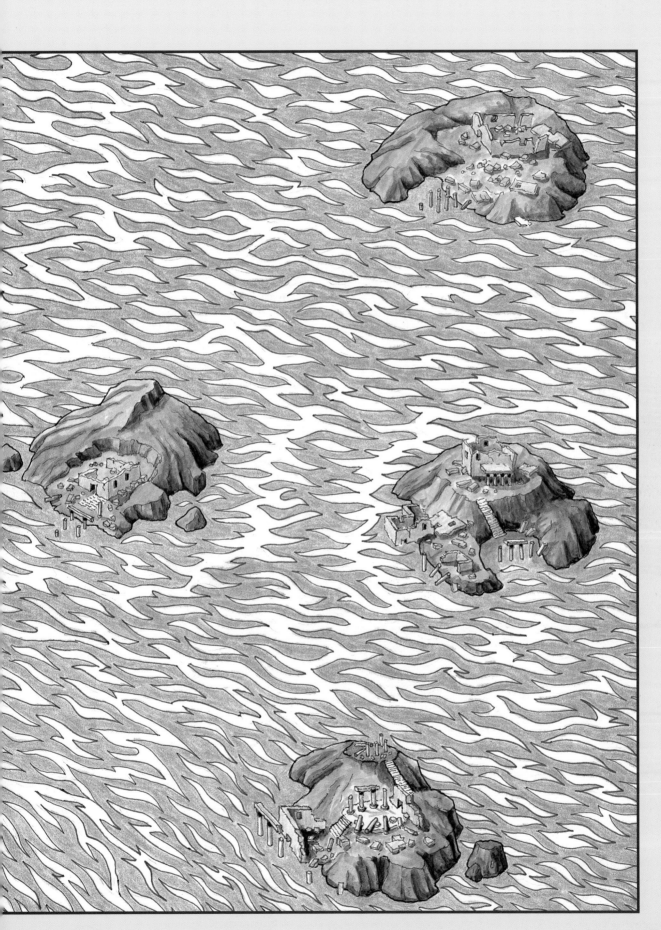

The City of Atlantis

There it is! Find a clear way to reach the city of Atlantis.

Start

End

Congratulations!

Thanks to your persistance and courage, you have been able to visit the sites of the great mysteries of the world and study and analyze what occurred there. You've had to go to dangerous places where great efforts by others in the past have failed. The going has not been easy, but you succeeded because you are the kind of person who never gives up. Now you need to make the results of your hard work known. The world will be eager to learn the results of your findings and put to rest once and for all the many unanswered questions surrounding these mysteries. Thanks.

If you had any difficulties along the way, you can refer to the solutions to the mazes on the following pages.

Cover Maze/Stonehenge

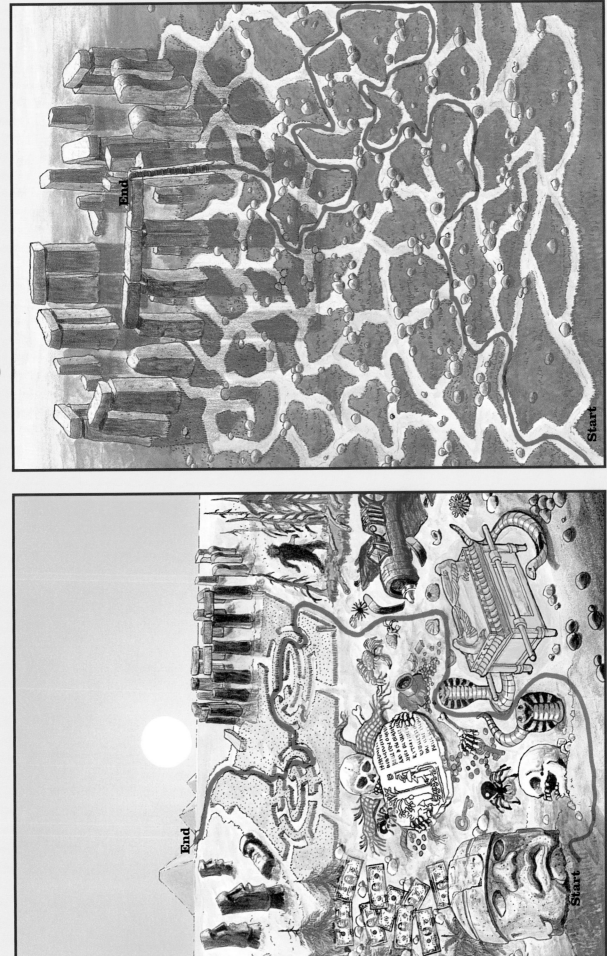

The Search for the Mayan "Rosetta Stone"

Start

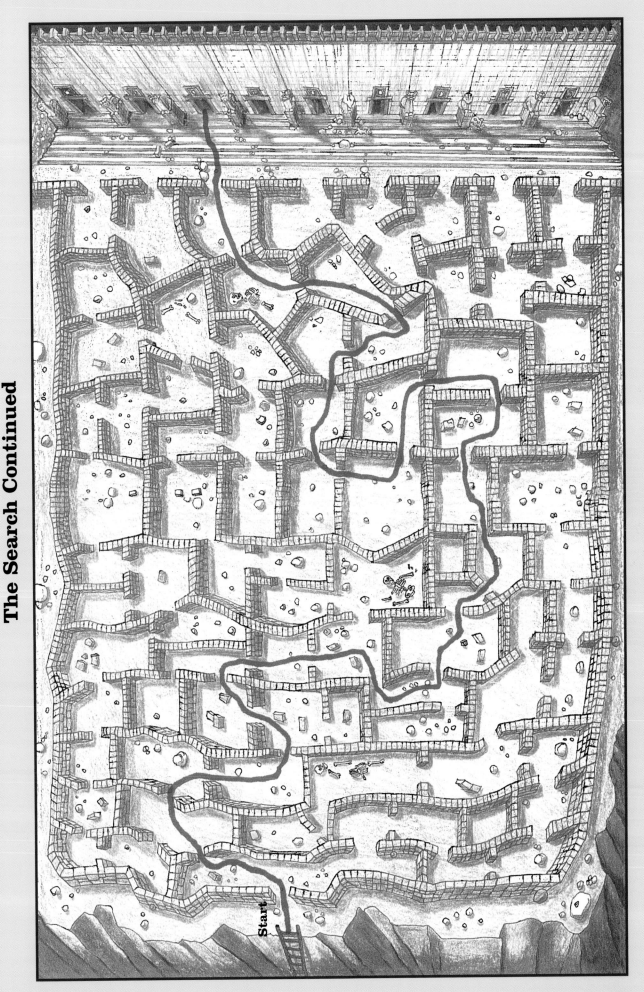

The Search Continued

Start

The Mayan "Rosetta Stone"

Start

End

The Olmec Head

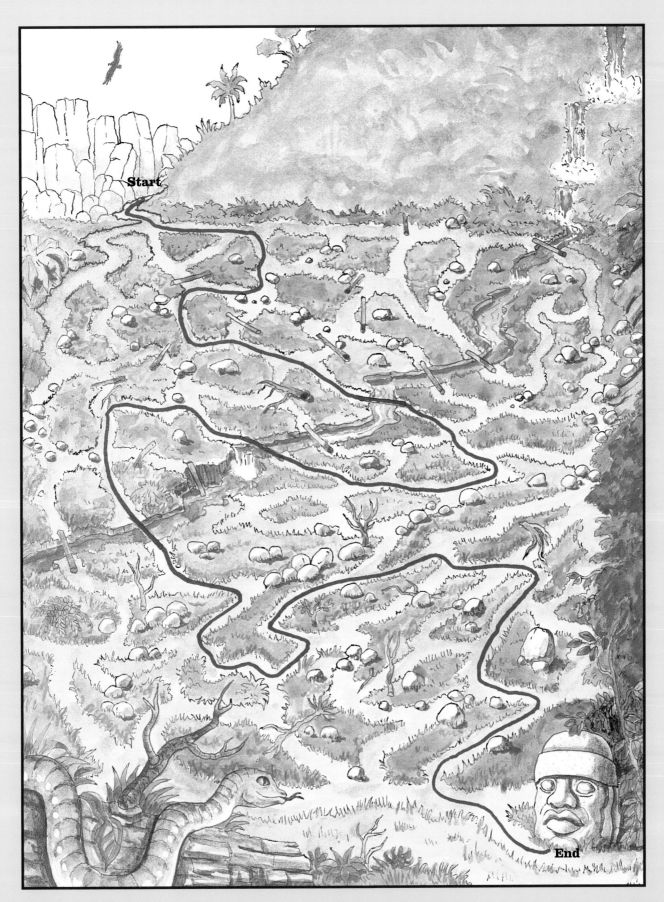

Start

End

Easter Island Sculptures

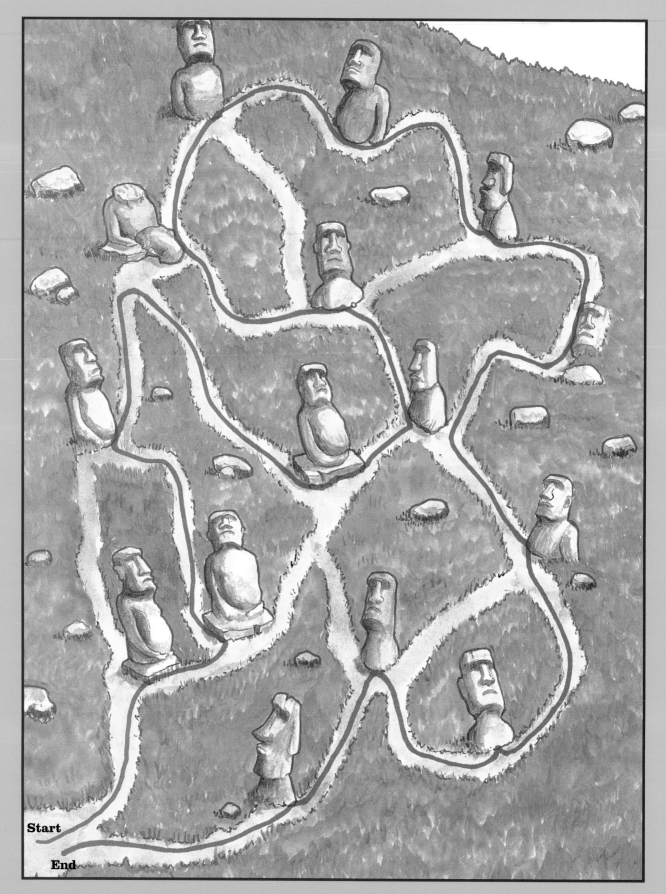

Start

End

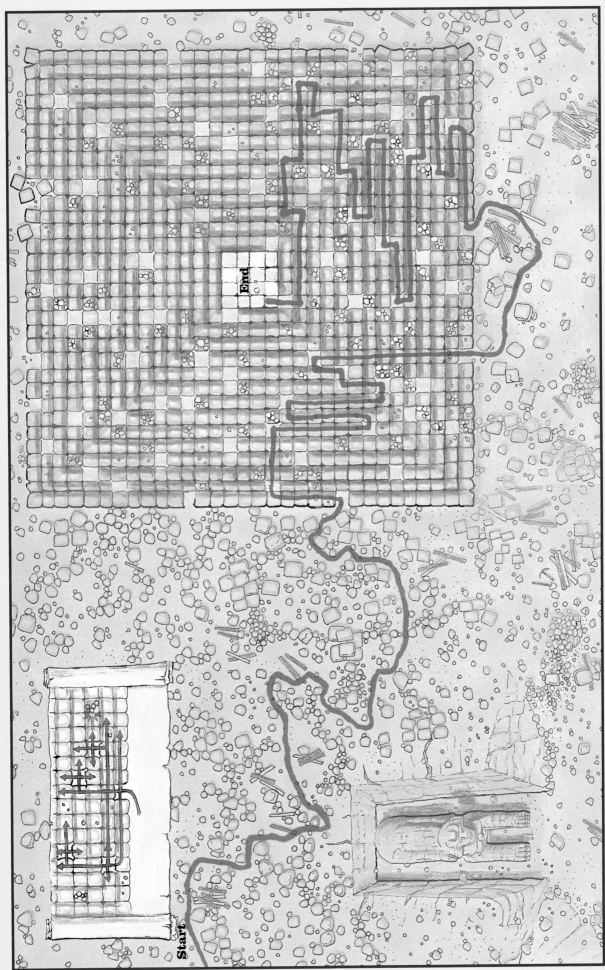

The Great Pyramid

Start

End

The Search for the Ark of the Covenant

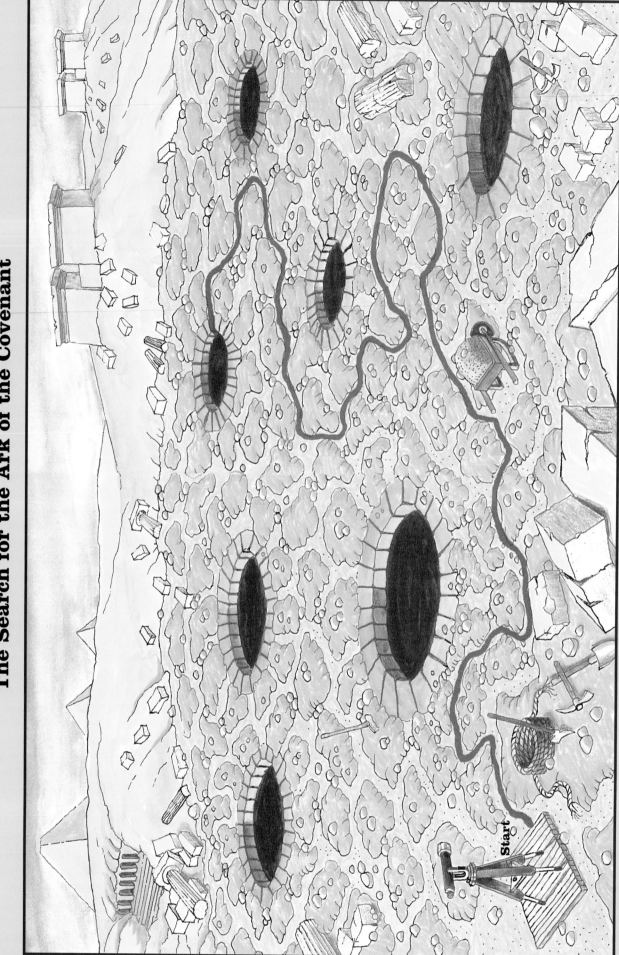

Start

The Ark of the Covenant

Enter the Money Pit

Start

The Money Pit Continued

End

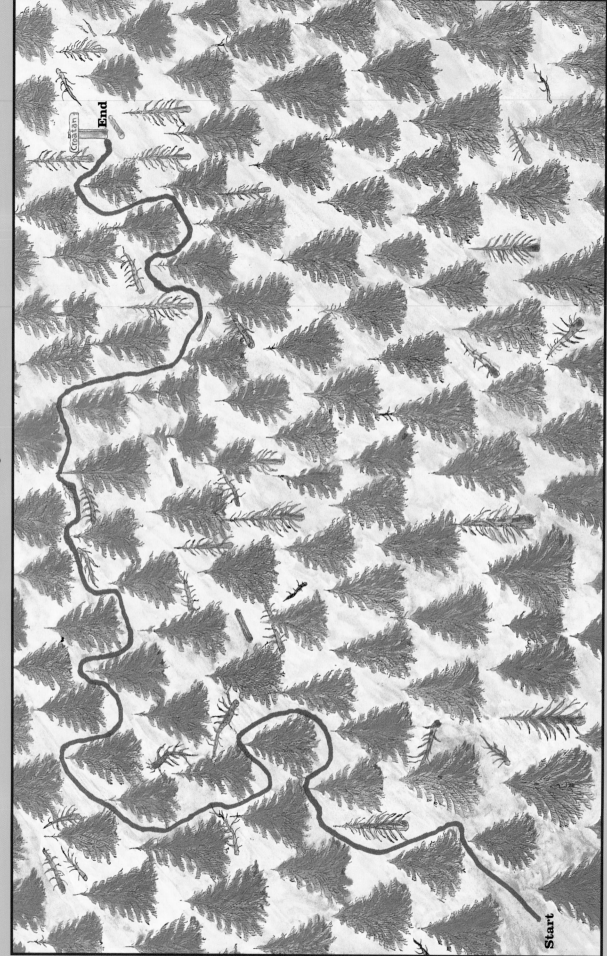

The Lost Colony of Roanoke

Croatian

End

Start

The *Mary Celeste*

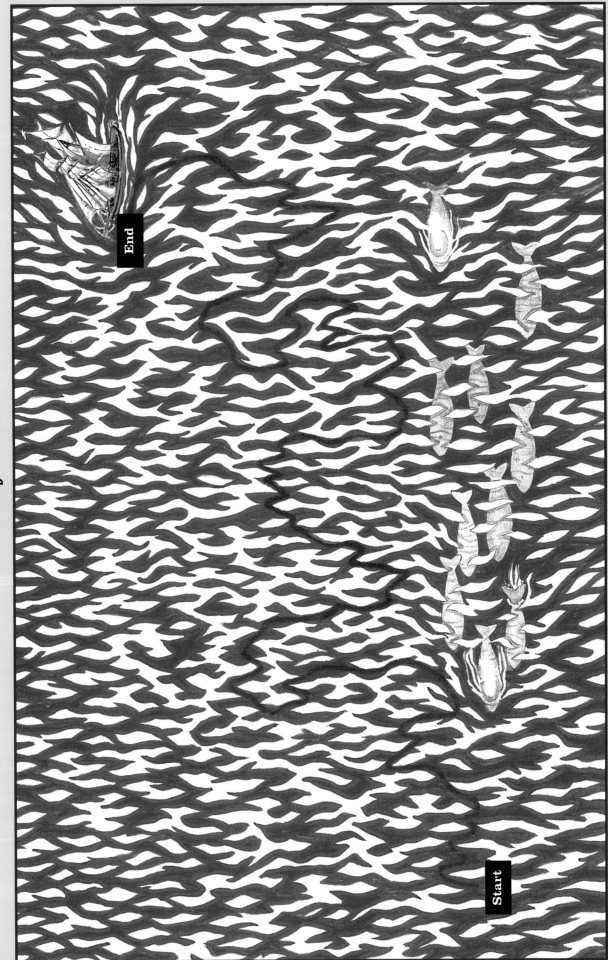

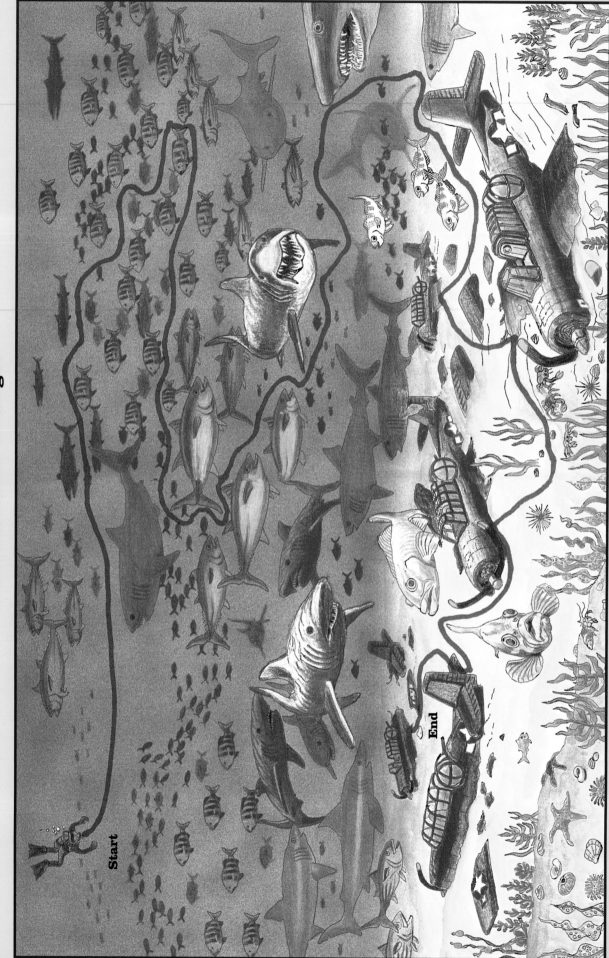

The Bermuda Triangle

Start

End

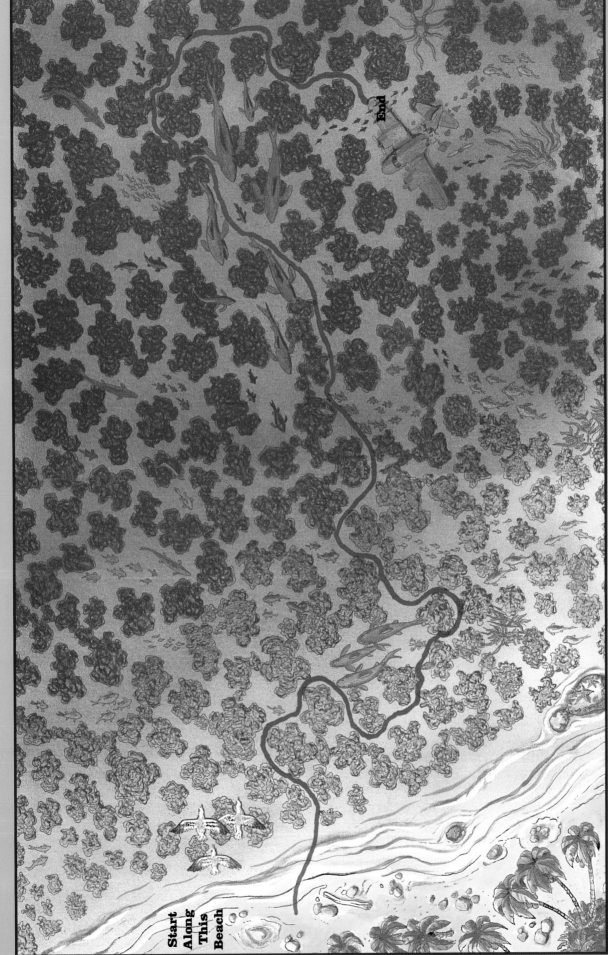

Amelia Earhart

End

Start
Along
This
Beach

Nessie

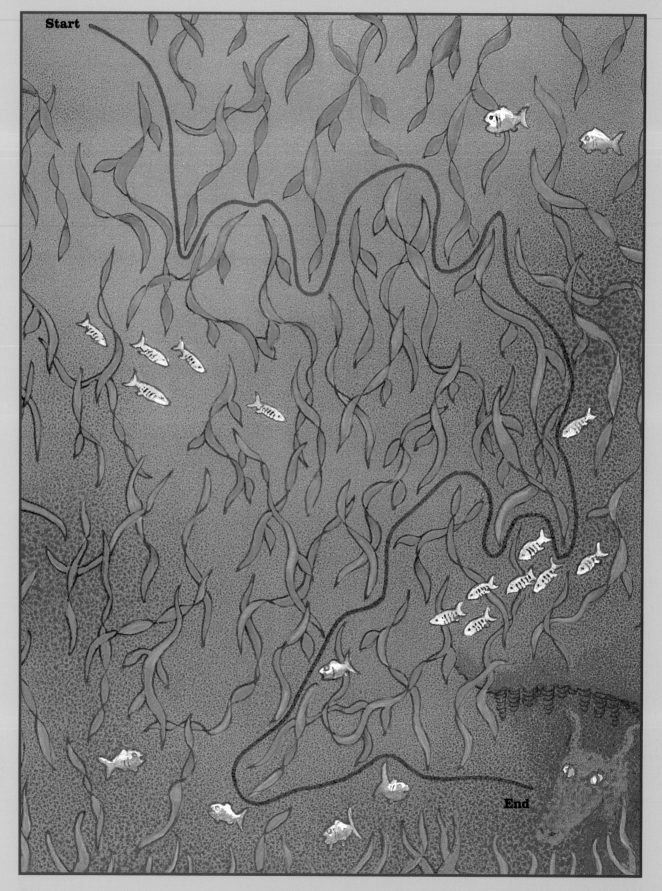

Start

End

Big Foot

Start

End

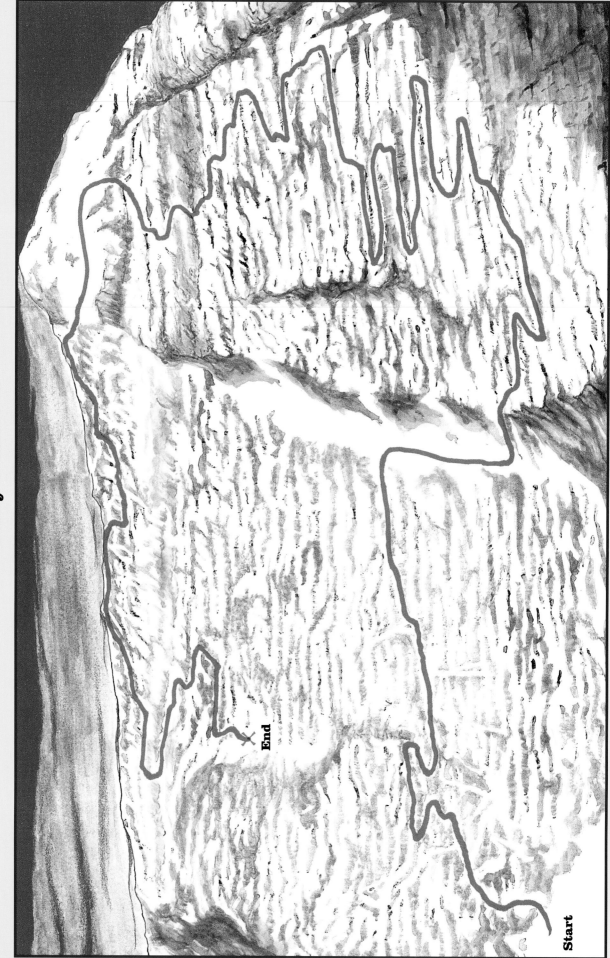

Start

End

The Yeti

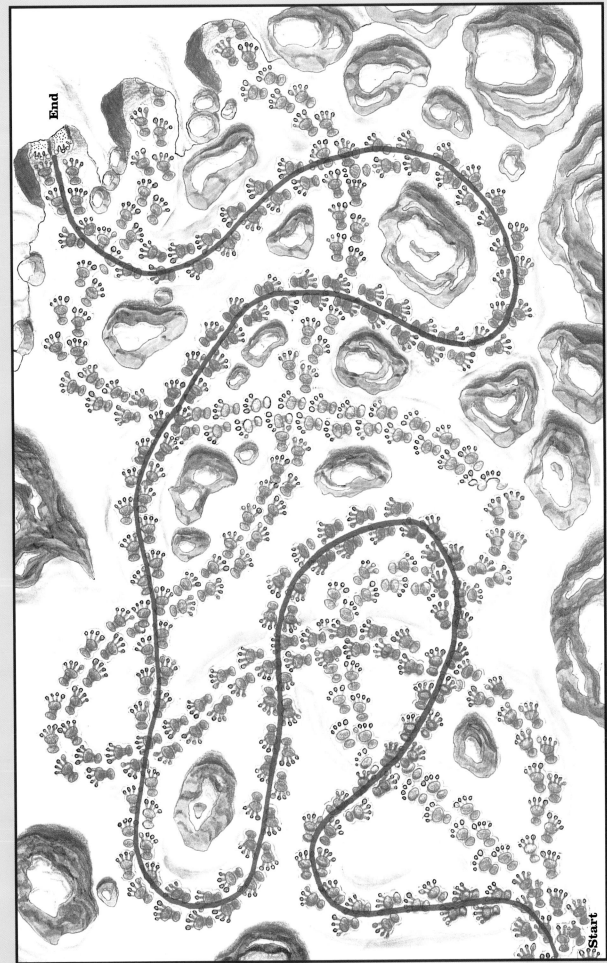

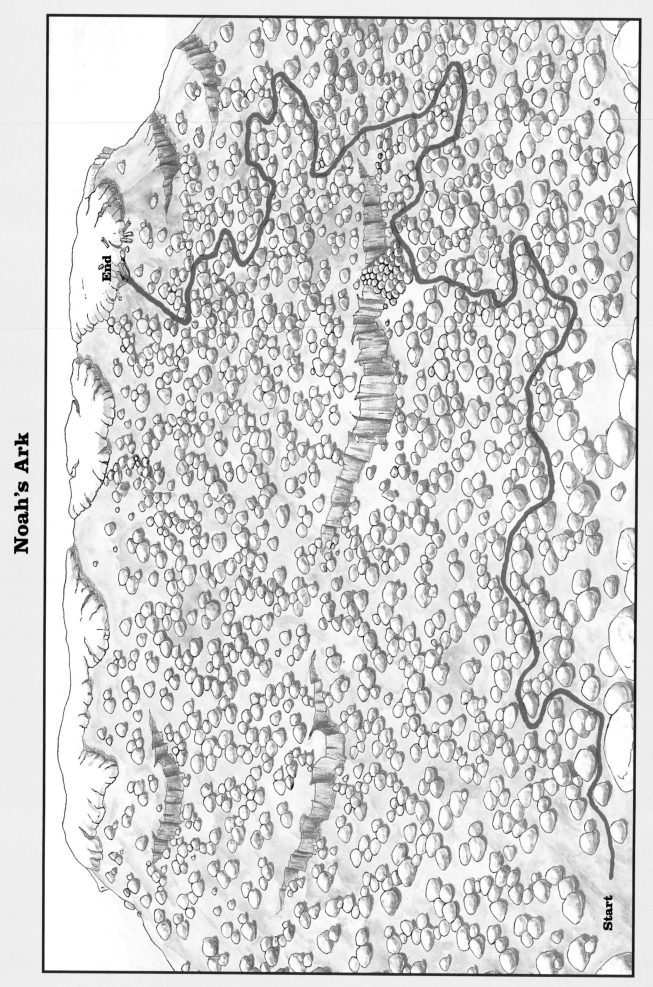

Noah's Ark

Start

End

Shangri-La

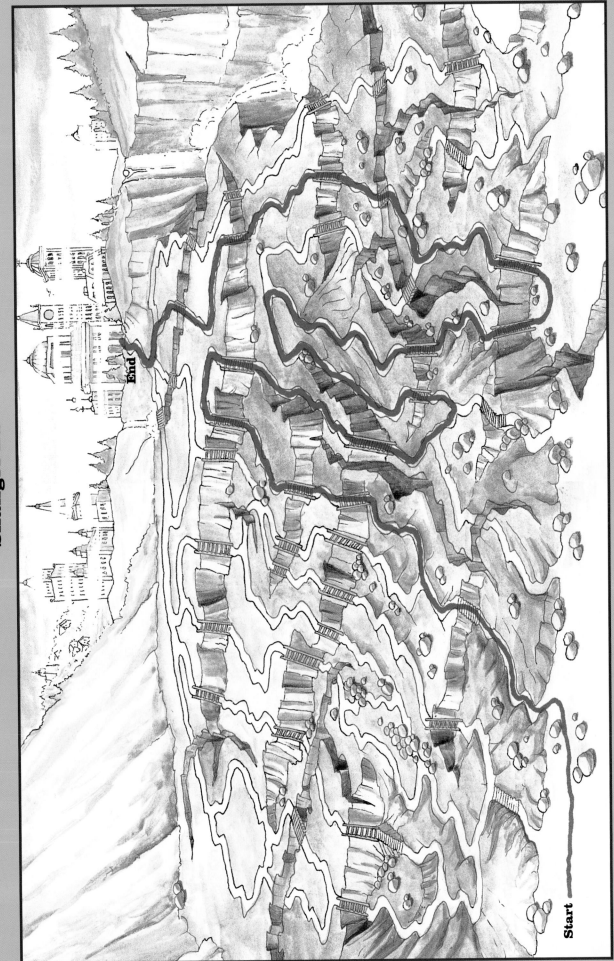

Roswell's UFO

Start

End

Crop Circles

D.B. Cooper

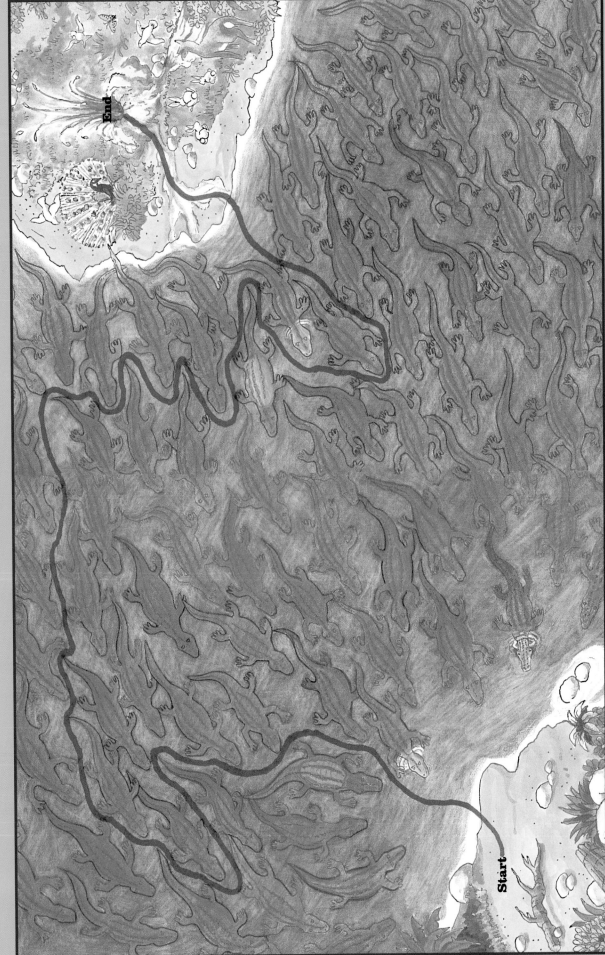

The Fountain of Youth

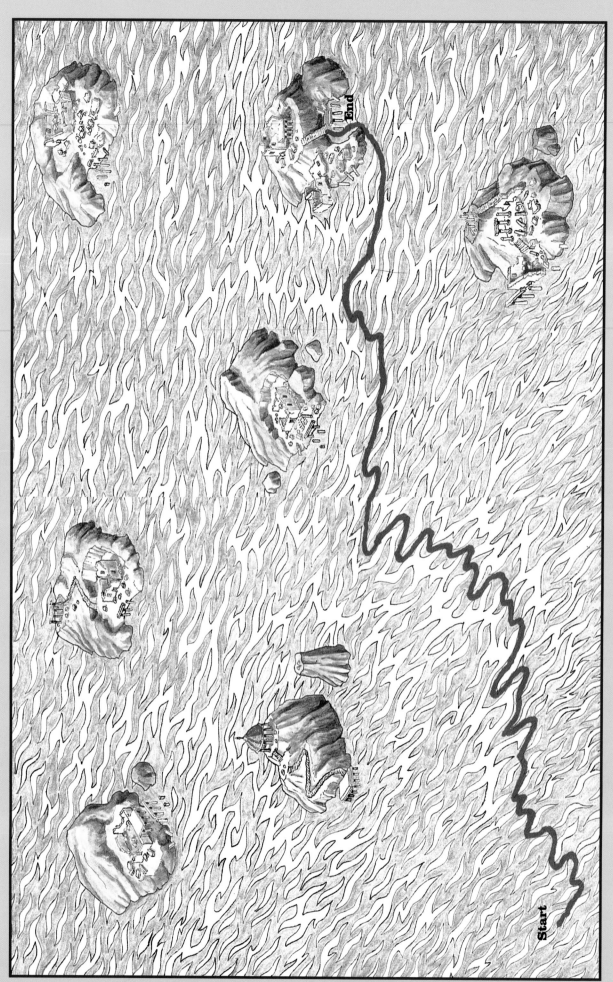

The City of Atlantis

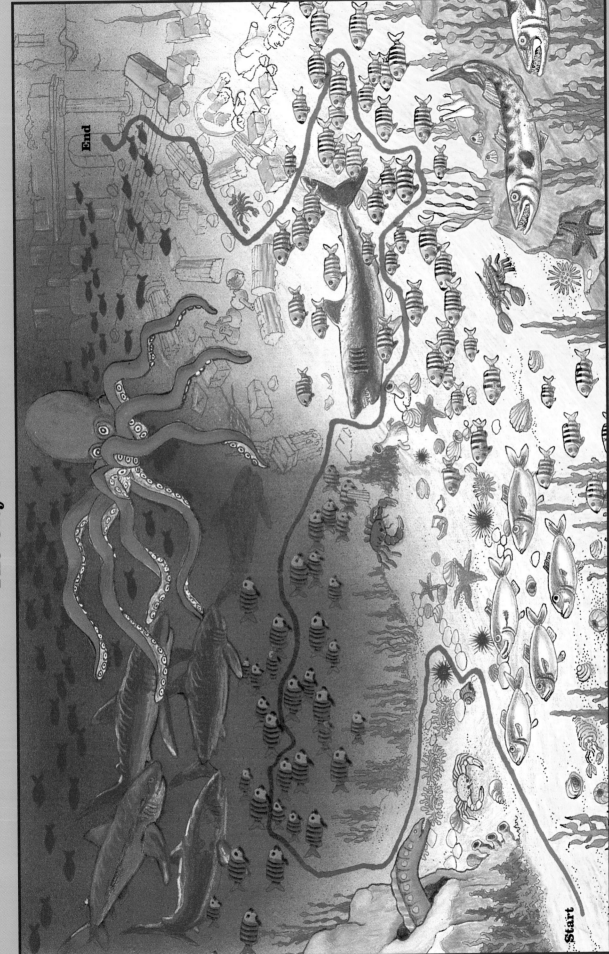

End

Start

Index

Page numbers in **bold** refer to answer mazes.

Ark of the Convenant, 6, 18–21, **60–61**

Atlantis Island, 6, 48–49, **78**

Bermuda Triangle, 5, 28–29, **66**

Big Foot, 6, 33, **69**

City of Atlantis, 50–51, **79**

Cooper, D.B., 5, 44–45, **76**

Crop circles, 6, 43, **75**

Earhart, Amelia, 5, 30–31, **67**

Easter Island, 5

Easter Island Sculptures, 15, **58**

Enter the Money Pit, 22, **62**

Flight 19, 5, 28–29, **66**

Fountain of Youth, 6, 46–47, **77**

Great Pyramid, 6, 16–17, **59**

Himalayas, 36–37

Howland Island, 30

Irvine, Andrew, 34

Leon, Ponce de, 6, 46

Loch Ness monster, 6, 32–33, **68**

Lost Colony of Roanoke, 24–25, **64**

Mallory's Camera, 34–35, **70**

Mallory, George, 34–35

Mary Celeste, 6, 26, 27, **65**

Mayan "Rosetta Stone," 8, 12, 13, **54–56**

Mayas, 6, 8–13

Money Pit, 22–23, **62–63**

Mount Ararat, 6, 38–39, **72**

Mount Everest, 34–35, **70**

Nessie, 6, 32–33, **68**

Noah's Ark, 6, 38–39, **72**

Noonan, Fred, 30

Oak Island, 6

Olmec Head, 14, **57**

Olmecs, 5

Pyramids, 5

Roanoke Island, 6, 24–25, **64**

"Rosetta Stone," 8–13, **54–56**

Roswell, 6

Roswell's UFO, 42, **74**

Search for the Ark of the Covenant, 18–19, **60**

Search for the Mayan "Rosetta Stone," 8–9, **54–55**

Shangri-La, 6, 40–41, **73**

Stonehenge, 5, 7, **53**

Yeti, 6, 36–37, **71**